Wabi Savvy

Melissa Lora

Wabi Savvy
Copyright © 2021 by Melissa Lora

All rights reserved. No part of this book may be reproduced or transmitted in any form or by any means, electronic or mechanical, including photocopying, recording, or by any information storage and retrieval system, without the express, written permission of the publisher or the author. The exception is reviewers, who may quote brief passages in a review.

ISBN: 978-1-7371915-0-6

Wabi Savvy

To everyone who never fits in, feels alone, unloved, rejected or misunderstood.

... I understand.

Contents

Year One "Commencement" 8

Year One "Separation" 9

Year Two "Papá" 10

Year Three "Sacrifices" 11

Year Four "Reconstruct" 12

Year Five "Don't go" 14

Year Six "Robbed" 16

Year Seven "Escape" 17

Year Eight "Reunited" 19

Year Nine "Short-lived" 20

Year Ten "Robbed" 22

Year Eleven "Déjà vu" 23

Year Twelve "Prey" 25

Year Twelve "New York" 27

Year Thirteen "Swan" 29

Year Fourteen "Edgar" 31

Year Fifteen "Stranded" 33

Year Fifteen "Rejection" 34

Year Sixteen "Escape" 36

Year Seventeen "Tripped" 38
Year Seventeen "Spiral" 40
Year Eighteen "Witness" 41
Year Nineteen "The One" 43
Year Twenty "Popped" 44
Year Twenty "Ungrounded" 45
Year Twenty-one "Unleashed" 46
Year Twenty-one "Unloved" 48
Year Twenty-two "Roommate" 49
Year Twenty-three "The Intern" 50
Year Twenty-four "Chopped" 52
Year Twenty-four "Pruned" 53
Year Twenty-five "The Climb" 55
Year Twenty-six "Mobbin'" 57
Year Twenty-six "Repeat" 59
Year Twenty-seven "Awakening" 61
Year Twenty-eight "Mirror" 63
Year Twenty-eight "Plunge" 65

Year One "Commencement"

Mom pushed for the deliverance
Of a being who was perceived as unwanted
Instinctively she crawled through the darkness
Inching closer to see the light

No words to pronounce that I was finally here
Instead, I released a discomforted cry
All eyes wandered to this foreign being
Oblivious to the path that awaits

"Melissa, is her name," she said
Ten pounds placed upon her chest
I imagine the warmth that connected us
As I took the nutrients from her breast

My survival is on her hands
She felt the pressure and closed her eyes
Thoughts rushed in 'of all the sacrifices she has to make'
It's day one of eighteen years leading to my independence
Let the countdown begin

Year One "Separation"

Anger fueled mom's veins
While blood rushed to mask her lost face
She didn't know then
that the impulse to grab the broom to inflict physical pain was
going to cause an effect.
The fear that dialed those 3 numbers.
The justice that reacted by removing the "threat".
But how an act of protection caused by ignorance
Instead create unprecedented destabilization?

Year one, and there's a chance
that there will be no salvation.

"Mami, where are you?"
She was surrounded by brittle bricks
Behind rusted metals
Consumed by emotions to be deemed regrettable
Goodbye, misguided big brothers
This is the beginning of our permanent separation.

Year Two "Papa"

The warmth of dad's chest
Permeates all over my flesh
as he carries me in between his furry arms.
The paternal presence that I will always crave.

The smile that says,
"Mi niña my child, you are safe".
The love that oozes subconsciously
Because I am the reflection of him
I carry the code that unlocks his tender and caring nature.

Child number three
I hoped to be his favorite creation
I uttered "Papá"
It was my first word to him.

A word that has grown to be meaningless
through the absence of him.

Year Three "Sacrifices"

Waking up alone
The moonlight shone past my mom's eyes
How can my child go on when she must rise at this time of night?
"I must pay the bills
I must leave you behind
The American dream is calling me
The money is all that I have".

Let's call Mamá
She will take care of you
You will be fine on her watch.

Transported through air
To a foreign land you once called home
Where you leave me to be on my own
With familiar and unknown faces.

As you walk away, I am yet to know
That your sacrifice of a greater good

Means that my mother is now gone.

Year Four "Reconstruct"

Mamá was stern
Demanding actions from all of us
with her rigid ways.
Controlling her surroundings
With each final word that was said.

"Tienes que tener pelo largo y enflaquecer. Ponerte en linea para enflorecer
One must have long hair and a small waist to flourish
she sometimes said.

She was my new mom
The only one I now have
The sting of the belt I had to get used to
With each whip that landed on my legs, back, and arms.

A baby bottle filled with water was handed to me to soothe my sorrows.
And with each cry ignored, I did as follows.

It was all to gain your attention
I still craved your affection.

A doll for me to play with got handed to me
Until it was time for me to eat.

Sleep
Eat
Escape
Whip

Repeat.

Year Five "Don't go"

I held Mamá's hand and clenched to the warmth that kept me safe
She let go and said to me:
"*La escuela es para aprender*
The school is for you to learn".
The rush of abandonment hit my nerves.

I begged for her to take me along
Pulled on her shirt with tears flooding my freshly ironed shirt.
"*Mamá, no te vayas! Perdon, me comportare bien!*
Mamá don't leave! I'm sorry, I'll behave!"
I cried hysterically
I hoped that she would alleviate the pain.

She consoled me with a hug
And then began to walk away
"*Who are they?*
And who is she?
Why are the rocks kept on the ground?"

Those were there for me to kneel on
And to feel the sun burn my skin.
Kneeling down, I stared at the chipping wall
Counting down the hour
Until I was free

Here comes the callous teacher
I must obey
We both stood in front of the flames hissing from the stove
Eyes widened with each step closer that I take
"Saca la lengua
Stick out your tongue" she said
Unwillingly, I did so with tears rolling down my cheeks.

She turned off the stove and hugged me
as the pee drenched my freshly ironed khakis.

Year Six "Robbed"

Standing silently in the patio
It was just the two of us
While my bound grandfather sat in the living room
watching TV with not a worry in mind.
"Did Papá know this about you?"
Such thoughts still cross my mind.

As you looked me in the eyes, whispering
"No digas nada. Don't say anything."
Threatening words to convince the naive
that I will be punished for being punished.

The roll of your tongue was foreign to me
Papá is right there... your best friend.
If he knows, he will come save me
He never stood up
He never looked up
Don't worry Papá,
I'll protect you
I know you are in pain
I won't say a word
Let's play your little game

Year Seven "Escape"

With each contrived encounter
Your lips lingered much longer on mine
And your undesirable touch
Became rougher on my fragile body
But I must not say a word

Today, I'll be dropped off at the airport
And maybe I'll be able to see a boarding plane
Before I leave, I must say goodbye.

To my family
My home
My promiscuous cat
Alas, I enter the plane and five hours later,
Mom is standing there
By the entrance.

She welcomes me with a warm hug and a loving kiss
"Tienes hambre. Are you hungry?" she asks
"Si. Yes." I said

Holding a strawberry milkshake in my hand
I stare out of the car's window
Mesmerized by endless industrial buildings and shiny bright lights.

I take another sip
With a satisfied smile
Knowing that I am free from your forbidden touch now
Knowing that I can speak freely now.

Year Eight "Reunited"

There's a tall muscular man seated in the living room
"Who is he?"
Mom answers:
"*Él es tu Papá!. He is your dad!*"
He embraces me while grinning as he looks at me
His brown almond shaped eyes look like mine
And so do his plump lips.

I now have a dad
And he's taking me on a road trip.
I sit inside his truck
With unfamiliar faces surrounding me
"*Ellos son tus dos hermanas y hermano. Dile hola.*
Those are your two sisters and brother. Say hi" he tells me.
I have siblings to play with? I ask.
We smile and giggle as we arrive at *Good Times*.

We are all having a good time
There's pizza
A busy arcade
And all the ice cream that I want!
I hope that this remains my new reality
And not a longing dream
I hope that he is as happy
As he has made me
I now have a dad.

Year Nine "Short-lived"

Mom's phone rings
Who can it be?
She picks up the call
And hangs up with a surprised grin.

"Your brother is coming to visit us!"
A big brother that I can't wait to meet.

For 21 days
We both played with my dolls
Ate at *Chili's*
And watched movies in 3D.

We opened our Christmas presents together
Took photos in Downtown with the Christmas trees
Her eyes twinkled when he was around.
It's been 7 years since you've been back in town

You were 10 then
Now you're 17.

It's been 21 days together
But today you take your leave.

When will you return?
She gave you a call once

Twice
Or maybe three times
You picked up and said
That you are too busy to come see us
We never saw you again.

Year Ten "Robbed"

As I rose from the shallow rest from one more night of mom's too-loud insensible bliss
The desire to search led to me standing and peeking into your vacant room
You weren't there… so the search began
Seeking dollar bills instead I found a folded bill
Perfectly hidden under the pretentious vase
Gently unfolding, I discovered a trace
A line not so straight and as white as snow
I knew then that the powder wasn't for my body
And it didn't belong in your nose
Speeding along to the toilet
The particles fell and swirled down the drain
The flushed mistake to avoid
Your secret became my secret
Hoped she won't notice
Hoped she won't know
That the bill under the burdened vase

Did not disappear on its own.

Year Eleven "Deja vu"

I'm going on a vacation
To the land that I once explored
I reunited with my dearest friend on the steps of her comforting home.

Oh the joys we were to share
Your estranged dad is coming to get us and drive us to the ice cream store.

"*Quiero helado de bizcocho en un cono.* I want a cake batter ice cream cone," I said.
"*Lo que tu quieras, mi amor.* Whatever you want, my love." he said.

Your dad is my dream come true
I wish he was my dad.
We drove to his foreign home
A beautiful landscape that had an open porch.

She ran to the bathroom, and we sat across from each other as we casually spoke
His eyes glimmered as he stared at my lips
Does he love me?
No. That's lust.

Unexpectedly his body rose, stood in front of me and asked for a kiss on the cheek
I tilted my head and met with his forbidden lips
The familiar feel of the tongue pushing uninvited into the mouth
The steps were heard loudly as she returned to her seat
I mustn't say a word.
Not now at least.

Her dad has filled her with incomparable joy
I won't be the thief of her bliss
As I departed from the van
One last kiss he stole again unwillingly.

"No digas nada. Te extrañaré, mi amor. Don't say a word. I will miss you, my love" was his goodbye.
A man I had wished to be my dad
Turned out to be a man I wished never to see
The land I once explored as my home
Is no longer a place for me.

I'm leaving this vacation today,
Back to safety.

Year Twelve "Prey"

As I look outside of the foggy window
A tall boy with baggy jeans and shirt looks my way
I am surrounded by screaming voices
And sounds of laughter
And then he says "You are so ugly and fat"
And everyone else looks my way.

His voice carries on in the background
And the growing ache in my chest remains suppressed
Can this bus hurry up?
I want to escape all the witnessing eyes which are burning my flesh
I hear the laughter of his friends
And those of others nearby.

Who is going to help?
Will I be saved?
I get off the bus and walk towards the brick building
The elevator couldn't rise any quicker
It is racing against my thoughts
I toss my bag on the couch
And the tears begin to roll down.

Why God? Why must I be punished?
Is there something that I have done?

I remain alone on the couch
I must not say a word

The next day arrives
And I stand at the bus stop, hoping the bus does not show up.

Year Twelve "New York"

It is another weekend trip to Manhattan
To visit mom's friends.
This time, my best friend is coming along
for a getaway from the mundane.

Their laughter can be heard from the living room
The overpowering music is easy to tune out as we joyfully play.

One sip
Then two puffs
One bottle has been emptied
Two new bottles are opened
And the tension began to rise.

Uncontrolled screaming and shouting drown out the music
The noise is coming from my mom
She's attacking her friend's husband
Her friend is standing between the two.

Now she must decide
Between my mom and him
A choice must be made soon..

"Get out now!" she speaks
Confused, we gather our bags
And then head towards the exit.

Here we are
Mom, me, and my friend
Standing outside the front door with the luggage in hand.

With nowhere to go, we walk as she remains incoherent
Screaming at us to march forth
The rain starts to pour
We stand under a sign
Empty streets at 3 AM
A taxi drives along
I desperately wave my hand begging for salvation
And a bearded man magically stops.

Shed aggressively pulls my hair to feel the pain that she carries
I quickly get in the cab and hope for him to drive off
We finally arrive in Queens
And safety opens the door.

Here we all lay
Counting down the minutes, for us to return home from the hellish getaway
The morning shines through the dull windows
As we wait for the bus to arrive.

Making our return,
She looks back at me and says
That she remembers everything
From the screams, the yells, and the hair pull
with a satisfied smile and a hateful stare.

Year Thirteen "Swan"

With each pound that was shed
The taunting lessened
The clothes fit baggier
And the teachers began to question

Am I being threatened?
Am I suffering at home?
"No" I said to both questions.
A diet was imposed on me
A magic pill
That worked as an appetite suppressant
The magic that shut him up
The magic that made my reality pleasant

I picked up the brush
Smearing the hue of pink on the lid
I picked up the pencil
Drawing a line to resemble a cat's eye
My lips were of red tint and cheeks of the color peach

I felt lightheaded
I needed food
I walked to the kitchen
A banana lay by the kitchen sink
I will eat half I tell myself
Half of it is all that I need

Then came the school bus
I walked in.
Then briefly I paused at the entrance
I looked his way and gave him a contented smile
Then took my seat
My reality was now pleasant

Year Fourteen "Edgar"

Mom thinks I'm going to a friend's house

But I get on the bus to meet you instead
The feel of cotton overpowers my mouth
And the words I utter can hardly be heard
I feel my knees weaken
With each step I take.

I stand in front of the store
Minutes later,
I see your face
I must have been blushing
As I flustered from your warm embrace
Being in your physical presence beats all those late Myspace messages.

Can this be real?

That you want to be with me
You. The popular handsome guy
You. Whose lips have turned purple
It must be the tobacco leaves.

"You're beautiful. You don't need makeup" he said.
So I washed the mask off
For your acceptance.

We hung out at your grandma's place
I never saw your grandma's face
And with each day,
I fell harder and craved your gentle touch
I longed for your desire to see me.
I longed for us to always stay in touch.

We sat on your grandma's couch,
  Laughing as we both watched *Get Rich or Die Trying*.
"Let's go upstairs," you said.
And then you laid in bed
Pants down
Waiting for me to touch you
"No, I don't want to." I said

The words that drifted us apart

Your hands I hardly felt
My hand was no longer held
You walked ahead as you dropped me off to the bus stop,
And then I read those last words from you:
"It's over. We can be friends".
My heart shattered into pieces
Realizing that lust is all you felt.

Year Fifteen "Stranded"

Awakened and not by a kiss
But by the scream coming from mom's voice
My name echoed in the air
I jump quickly to her rescue
There he has her pinned down by the neck holding it as she choked
He glances my way and immediately lets go
And knocks get heard from the door.

Knock! Knock!
"Who's there?" I said
"The police. Open up".

As I open the door
I am brushed to the side
for an the unwarranted search
Chaos surrounds me
As pounds of white dust get found in his drawer

Now they are coming to find me
DSS is at our front door
I meet the judge and he likes me
Estranged sister to the rescue
Estranged dad is here too
While you sit behind rusted metals
Waiting and hoping for a judge to like you too.

Year Fifteen "Rejection"

A new start for me with Dad and his family
I have brothers now
And we all get to play video games
I have a dad again
And we get to spend time again
I am not alone now
I even like my stepmother too
I can get used to this
Being here with you

Who are you, dad?
What's your favorite color?
What do you like to do?
I watch you play chess on your own
Where are your friends?
My dad must be smart
Maybe I'll take after him

The day comes
You tell me to pack
You tell me you are dropping me off at my cousin's house

Why dad?
Why don't you want me dad?
I think I should beg

Maybe then I can stay
Longer than a few days
Am I really your daughter?

My dad, the donor
I now know who you are.

Here I stand alone
again.

Two weeks later
Mom has been released
We are reunited
Again.

Year Sixteen "Escape"

Late night shift at Walgreens
I walk along a sketchy vacant street
Mind adrift wondering:
What am I to eat?

I hear the tires swerving
of the black car that blocks my path
A dreaded man stepped out and said "Get in the bomboclat car!"

I smell the cognac on his breath and my heart drops
I can hardly breathe
I look around and only the two of us are standing there.

Who is that in the car?
It is a bearded man staring into oblivion
Help! Help! Can anyone hear me?
Those were my unspoken thoughts.

This is it
This is how it is going to end
My clothes will be stripped away
And I will no longer be free
My purity will be taken away
My world as I know it,
will no longer exist.

"I said get in the fucking car!" he shouts
With haste, he drops his phone
And the fear in me intensifies
"Pick that shit up!" he screams again.

Should I say no?
Or pick it up and throw it at his head?
I reach for the phone under the car
I toss it at his bulging chest
I start to run against the gush of wind

The pizza shop is open
I hurriedly open the door and walked in
I stand there
Watching him park across the street.

As I plan my escape
He looks away,
And I run away.

I swear beneath my breath
I will never walk alone at night again.

Year Seventeen "Tripped"

Navigating the strange waters in Maine
Sailing into the unknown
I have been away for weeks
Surrounded by strangers
Whom I have now come to know

Seven days climbing the Kibby mountain
Being pulled back by the backpack's load
There are no showers
Three more days until I am back home

Here I stand by the tent
I hear my name going back and forth
"She's the nicest" she said
"Such great teeth," he said
"But the bloody mess can't be ignored."
I think they know that I have heard them
They wear surprised faces as I open the tent
to lay on sticks and stones

Today's the day I get to shower
That must mean too that I get to go home
Mom is standing at the entrance
Waiting for me
Telling me that she has a surprise for me.

She opens the door
And there he is standing
That one that shocked you
And separated you from me.

Year Seventeen "Spiral"

Finally, I made it back home
How I longed to talk to my beloved

I opened AOL Instant Messenger and sent him a text
Telling him how much I have missed him
He answered back with a reply
That lets me know it wasn't mutual
My presence didn't matter
The joy I felt before dwindled
With tears rolling down my face.

I don't have him
Or anyone to love.

It's 7 AM
"Time to get ready for school"
Mom yelled.
Every other missed day turned into weeks
There's nothing there for me.

Take your scholarship
Take your dreams
Take your power
I just want all this to end
There is nothing left for me.

Year Eighteen "Witness"

The basketball rolled down the stairs
I grabbed it swiftly as the sun glared
There were voices coming from the porch
Casual conversations about lighting up the held blunt.

"I'm going to the park" I said
They decided to tag along
And with each step I took
A dribble was heard

A hooded man ran behind me
Down the trail he went
Maybe he is in a rush?

Another dribble was heard
His black hoodie on a summer day
Is all that I can remember
He stood behind me
With his arm stretched out
The silver gun released a bullet
Missing his target.

He tried again
Another bullet hit the pavement
The scent was carried by the wind to my nose

Should I stay or should I go?
The ball tugged under my arm
I ran up the steep hill.

The hill fought back
But my legs can't give up.

I am the witness to the demise
I must hide
With each step that I took
I got closer to the top
I made it to them.
And we all watched
As the hooded man walked back home.

Year Nineteen "The One"

I found him online
You were hers
Yet to be mine.

I didn't care
About who said what
A friend request that led to an awaited message
She's now a thing of the past.

The butterflies in my stomach fluttered when our eyes met
The sparks flew between us
This was meant to be
The missing piece to my puzzle
The hero that was here to save me

Clinging to your love
To the potential the two of us had
This was it
It's like a fairytale of two teenagers
Growing old together
Of two souls coming into a union

Finally,
The one.

Year Twenty "Popped"

The high that overwhelmed my mind
of dark thoughts of him and her flirting.
Dings of text messages sent back and forth
With slight smirks hidden between the lines.

The high that laid me down on a carpeted floor
With him laying behind me
Caressing what was yet to be explored
The swift movements that triggered the sensation
Unconsented penetration
Taking my purity…

The high that led to shedding many tears
For losing what I had held on to for so long
"You don't even love me!" I said.
This is so wrong
And there you were professing that you were in love
on a carpeted floor.

Year Twenty "Ungrounded"

Mom knocks on my bedroom door
Walks in and says to me:
"This is our last month. Find where to go".

My house is no longer my home
Time is ticking
I have nowhere to go.

As I cling to his body for safety,
I whisper "Please don't go"
The ground beneath me now shakes
3 more days to go.

I leave with him
And we drive to his grandma's house
With a bag full of clothes
A few shoes and scarfs
Everything else goes.

We walk up the stairs
To a room with a couch, a dresser and closet
In silence, we both lie there
It's me
It's him
It's both of us and this futon
Against the world.

Year Twenty-one "Unleashed"

The crickets surrounded us
In a tent with familiar bodies
He made a comment
And I was quick to anger

Making my way to his mom's parked car
I searched for peace
But I found torment in his nearing voice
"Get out!" He yelled.

I stood across to be shoved as his enemy
The love that enchanted me was now gone
My dreams had been shattered
And the illusion of us growing old together vanished
I don't recognize who we are anymore.

The getaway that led to my get away as the tension grew unbearable
His rooted rage now replaced love
The separation that became cemented
When he made the choice to keep driving straight
Instead of stopping home.

The key that flew in the air
As I exited the vehicle
Signaling that the key to your heart is now yours

It pained to know that this was the end
And now the feeling has returned
The feeling of me being alone

Year Twenty-one "Unloved"

What is it that I must do for me to be loved?
I feel the ache in my chest.

The realization that we are not right for each other
leads to drowning in my sorrows
Sedated with the liquid poison
Listening to the songs that reflect the internal horror.

I'm clouded with thoughts
That I am not good enough
No matter the makeup
No matter the weight loss
Rejection remains prominent

I begged for him to stay
Where is my salvation?
I don't want anyone's attention
I want to fade into the abyss
I want to forget that love exists
Because love is not for me
Love is not for me.

Year Twenty-two "Roommate"

Now here we are
Mom and I
Sharing one bed.

I lay on the right and she, on the left
There is one tiny closet to share
The privacy we once had
vanished into thin air.

The shared kitchen is filled with smoke
The smell of shisha penetrates the air
I pull on the rope to inhale the high
I pick up the rum to suppress the cry.

The music fills the room
to block the noise that's buzzing in my thoughts
The lack of stability
Is like walking on water
and I drown with each cup.

Here we are
Her and I
In one bed
In this new reality
I must step up to the plate
The parent-child role has become reversed.

Year Twenty-three "The Intern"

I dropped a class and I sat with guilt in bed
The phone rang and I heard the voice of a saint

Can this be heaven sent?
"I have a few questions for a job role".
An internship to replace the class I couldn't bear to take

I hung up and left with a scheduled interview with him
Only metered parking on the streets
I have one quarter
That's not enough
I open the door and walk in
I speak with him, her, and two more.

Three hours later, I leave
A $40.00 ticket awaits me on my windshield
A few days later,
I hear a ding.

It's an email with an offer
Is this really happening?
I'll make $17.00 an hour,
I breathe a sigh of relief.

Filled with joy
I reply with an "I accept" and hit sent
The change that I desperately need comes.

First day arrives
Same faces greet me
We sit in a circle
As I stand fully to realize my dreams.

Year Twenty-four "Chopped"

Sitting on the salon chair
Hair matted
I can feel their eyes as they stare
Silver scissors in stylist hand
Chops one strand, and then two strands.

A piece of me now lays on the floor
And tears begin to shed
A reflection of neglect
Of the sacrifice of self.

For him
For her
And all others
Of the shame that I wear
And the silence between me and the hairdresser
Says what needs to be heard.

The cry for help to cut off all the burdens
That I have carried to the salon chair.
A new style
A new beginning
A reflection that I have achieved a milestone
As I get ready to cross the graduation stage.

Year Twenty-four "Pruned"

I spent the most time with her
Singing in the kitchen
Making up dance moves
Sharing woes during our lows
A dependency that came with blurred lines
Not knowing if you were me or if I was you.

Here I am now
Ready to cross the graduation stage
An empty chair
For my best friend

Where are you?
Where are you during my real high?

I want to share this moment with you
She decided not to show up
My system with no support.
The unbalanced friendship
I give and you take some more

The system is out of order
It's time to throw it away
There I am
Crossing the stage

an empty chair still remains.
For who no longer is the best
For who no longer is my friend.

Year Twenty-five "The Climb"

Assigned Task
Another Task
Work messages sent during class
I can focus
I can pass
Another raise
More tasks.

Less time to focus
I can't pass
I drop one class
Then two
Third class.

Another raise
More time spent on their dreams
Even less time spent on mine
What is my dream?
What do I want?
I dared to speak
But a pushback replied

One more task finished
For them to take the shine
Blur out my name

My idea is now theirs
It is no longer mine.

Year Twenty-six "Mobbin'"

I trusted you
I told you things others did not know
I mean, *how could you?*
I was nice to you,
even with your flaws and all.

But the envious nature took over
and you had to do the undoing
My reputation is now in your hands
Do you think you can bring it to ruins?

Oh no, you will learn
That love can quickly turn into hate
The lever gets pulled
anger fueling my veins

My eyes darken
you will feel my pain
I will distort your reality
Make you fear the unknown
Sitting there crying for help when paranoia is at your door.

I trusted you
But not again
A lesson learned

You lost a friend
But I gained strength

Year Twenty-six "Repeat"

A beautiful creature that you are
I saw your potential and I fell madly for that
What is this strong sensation that I feel inside?
Could you be the one I have been waiting for all this time?

Those illusions were shattered when my shell wasn't up to par
The sting of rejection from you spread viciously across my heart
"I'm sorry. I didn't mean it." He said.
Words coerced to entrap
With each day that passed,
I was kept at bay
Until we finally met.

I opened the door and nerves got a hold of his logic
We laid in bed and I felt his body relax
We briefly saw eye to eye
There was promise in his eyes.

Before you walked out the door
We shared half a hug
Next day he was imprisoned
Two more weeks passed
And I was kept at bay again

Asked me to be your girlfriend
Clinging to your potential,
I said yes.
Released from jail to go to a program
Three more weeks that I won't be seeing you again.

"It's not me, it's you," I said
I chose to walk away
The phone rings
And rings
And rings.

All calls have been blocked
Now it's him who will remain at bay.

Year Twenty-seven "Awakening"

Chaos surrounds me
As my reality shifts and fear kicks in
The lockdown that brought it all to a halt
The invisible threat
That lingers in the air and surfaces now and again

One death
Two deaths
Hundreds more are dead abroad
I lie wondering
Am I living to live?
Am I working to die?
What is my dream?
Is my purpose to be free or to simply survive?

Hours remain until my air trip to Aruba
Email gets received carrying unwelcome news
News that shattered my hope of escape
Saying that the borders have been closed.

The trip to Aruba faded into the abyss
I turn the shower knob
And the water rises
As my body sinks.
I close my eyes

And count to four
Letting out a sigh
All I want is to be at peace.

Year Twenty-eight "Mirror"

When our eyes met
he was hunched over.
Flipping pages of his favorite tiger
And I knew then,
It was emotional pain that was blocking his pure heart.

Lack of attention
Lack of affection
Being neglected and rejected
for being who you are.

I saw me in him
And as he bit into my shoulder,
I shielded him from those judgmental eyes
I can't protect him from the pain
From the inhumane and selfish acts
or from his mom and dad.

And with no words
he warned me
That it was time for me to go.

I'm freeing myself for him
so he can free himself too.
The unconditional love

Will remain in your heart
And in mine too
I love you my favorite buddy
This is from me to you.

Year Twenty-eight "Plunge"

My two weeks are up
The jitters have kicked in
My mind races with myriad thoughts
I can't do it
Yes, I will!

A contradictory world I find myself in
I try to close my eyes
But the fear won't let me sleep

Is this the right thing for me?
Am I worthy of pursuing my dreams?

I can't do it
Yes, I will!

I take one pill
Some sleep aids
To stop the fight in the mind.

My body is slowly caving in
I pick up the pencil
And I start to write.

I can't do it
Yes, I will!

I am on the last page
Ending the stanza
For a new beginning
He said
She said
They all said I couldn't do it.

And I say
"Yes, I will."

I Am Here.

Email: Melissalorallc@gmail.com
Youtube Channel: To Whom it May Concern
Life Coaching Services: www.Melissalora.com

www.ingramcontent.com/pod-product-compliance
Lightning Source LLC
Chambersburg PA
CBHW072208100526
44589CB00015B/2434